I0834238

**Two Houses, One Lonely Broken Heart**


Published by Glorybound Publishing, Camp Verde, AZ
SAN 256-4564
Published in the United States of America
1st Edition
ISBN 978-1-60789-376-9 1-60789-376-2
Copyright data is available on file.
Olivares, Janet, 1955-
Two Houses, One Lonely Broken Heart /Janet Olivares
Includes biographical reference.
1. Self-Help 2. Child Counseling
I. Title

www.raphaccc.org
*www.gloryboundpublishing.com*



Understand this book is not intended as a substitute for consultation with a licensed practitioner. Please consult with your own physician or health care specialist regarding the suggestions and/or recommendations in this book. The use of this book implies your acceptance of this disclaimer. Thank you.

# *Two Houses, One Lonely Broken Heart*

Divorce through the eyes of a ten-year-old

BY DR. JANET OLIVARES

Glorybound Publishing
Camp Verde, Arizona USA
in the year 2026

# Table of Contents

# How to Use This Book

This book is written through the eyes of a 10-year-old child so you can better understand how everyday behaviors, tone, routines, and communication patterns affect children.

It is not written to blame.
It is written to build awareness.

Read it as an invitation not a verdict.

### 1. Read Slowly and Reflect

Most parents read one chapter at a time and pause before moving forward.

After each chapter, consider:

• What did the child notice?
• How did adult behavior shape the child's feelings?
• What small change could I make this week?

Growth happens in small adjustments, not dramatic overhauls.

### 2. Focus on What You Can Control

This book is not meant to compare homes or evaluate the other parent.

Instead, focus on what is within your control:

• Your tone
• Your consistency
• Your follow-through
• Your emotional regulation

Children benefit most when at least one home is steady.

### 3. Do Not Use This Book as Evidence

This is important.

This book should not be used to:

- Collect evidence
- Assign fault
- Argue custody
- Criticize your co-parent

Children feel safest when adults use insight to grow — not to compete.

### 4. Apply One Small Change at a Time

Choose one behavior to practice each week.

For example:

- Keep transitions calm and brief
- Repair quickly after conflict
- Maintain predictable routines
- Pause before responding when upset

Small, steady changes create long-term safety.

### 5. Use the Reflection Sections

Each chapter ends with four prompts:

- What I Saw
- What It Did to Me
- What I Learned
- What This Story Shows

These are designed to increase insight not guilt.

Take your time with them.

### 6. Keep the Focus on the Child

Children do not need perfect parents.

They need steady ones.

Your child benefits when you:

- Stay calm
- Keep your word
- Protect them from adult conflict
- Allow them to love both homes freely

Safety grows through consistency.

### 7. This Is a Tool for Growth, Not Judgment

You may feel sad, defensive, hopeful, encouraged, or emotional while reading.

All of that is normal.

Growth often begins with discomfort, but it does not end there.

It is not too late to create a safer experience for your child.

And even one steady adult can change the emotional climate of a home.

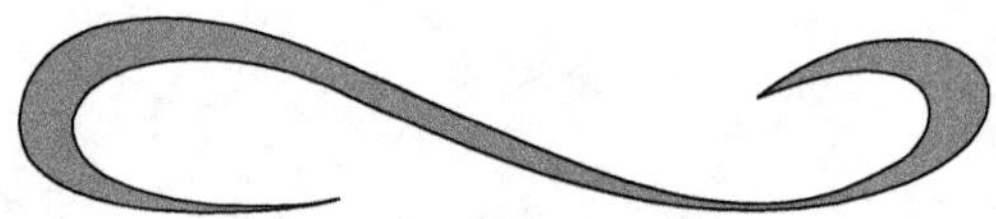

# Author's Note: About the Homes in This Book

This book is written from the perspective of a child experiencing life in two households after separation or divorce.

The homes described in these pages are not meant to represent "good" parents and "bad" parents." They reflect patterns that often emerge in emotionally charged or high-conflict co-parenting situations.

In many custody arrangements, one home may feel more structured while the other feels more permissive. This is rarely about love or intention. It is often shaped by guilt, fear of losing connection, or a desire to compensate for the pain of separation.

Professionals sometimes refer to this dynamic as a "Disneyland home," where rules are relaxed and routines shift in an effort to keep children happy. While understandable, these differences can unintentionally create confusion and emotional strain.

Children do not experience this as generosity or freedom.
They experience it as unpredictability.

The purpose of this book is not to judge either household. It is to help adults understand how children experience differences in tone, consistency, emotional regulation, and repair between homes.

Most parents love their children deeply. This book begins with that assumption.

It simply invites reflection on how stress, guilt, conflict, or unresolved hurt may shape parenting behaviors — and how small, steady changes can restore a child's sense of safety.

It is not too late to create that safety.

# Prologue: When We Were All Still Here

I am ten.

Before everything changed,
we all lived in one house.

It wasn't perfect.
But it was ours.

Mornings started the same way.

Someone made coffee.
Someone reminded us to hurry.
Someone forgot something by the door.

My sister sat at the table, swinging her legs.
My brother complained about school.

I knew where everyone was.

That mattered.

At night, I could hear doors.
I could hear voices.
I could tell who was at home just by the way it sounded.

I didn't think about it.

I just felt safe.

Weekends had routines.

We went places.
We stayed home.
We argued sometimes.
We laughed a lot.

No one whispered.
No one avoided eye contact.
No one told us to wait in our rooms.

Nothing felt hidden.

Then one day,
something changed.

Not loud.
Not dramatic.

Just… missing.

And I didn’t know yet
that missing can feel heavier
than noise.

# The Day Someone Was Gone

One Tuesday morning, I woke up and Dad wasn't there.

His clothes were gone.
Mom was crying.

There was:

No goodbye.
No explanation.
No warning.

The house felt quieter —
but not calm.

No one was talking.
When they did, they stopped when we walked in.

My sister asked,
"Where did Dad go?"

No one answered right away.

My brother went to his room.
He shut the door.

I stayed in the kitchen.

I waited.

No one told us what was happening.
No one said it would be okay.
No one told us anything except we needed to go to school.

That was the day I learned something.

Sometimes adults leave —
and kids are left with silence.

And silence is heavy.

Everything changes.

At first, Dad said he was staying somewhere else for a while.

Then he moved into a new house.

There was a woman named Stormy.
He said she was a friend.

We went to the park.
We had picnics.
We did fun things.

He seemed happy.

Mom's friend Ozzie started coming by when we were with her.
At first it was just visits.
Then he stayed longer.

Before I knew it, he didn't leave.

And one day I realized something else had changed.

We didn't just have one house anymore.

We had two.

I didn't know it yet,
but this was the last time
everything felt the same.

# PART I

## The Child's Voice

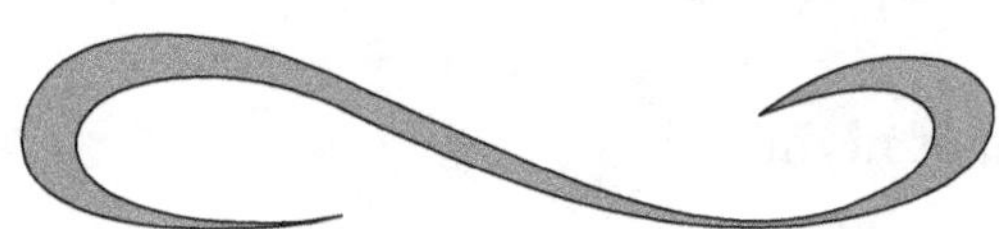

# Chapter 1
# Two Houses

I am ten.

I live in two houses now.

I did not choose this.
It just happened.

There are three of us kids.

My brother is fifteen.
He wears headphones a lot.
He acts like he does not care.
But he notices everything.
He remembers what adults promise — and what actually happens.

My sister is five.
She carries a stuffed animal everywhere.
She asks the same questions again.
She cries when voices change or doors close too fast.

I am in the middle.

I see things.
I hear things.
I remember things.
I think about them at night.

One house belongs to Mom and Ozzie.
The other belongs to Dad and Stormy.

Both houses have beds.
Both houses have food.
Both houses say they love us.

And I believe them.

But they do not feel the same.

At Mom and Ozzie's house, mornings start quietly.

The dog, Max, waits by the door.
The cat, Blue, sleeps on the couch.

Someone makes coffee.
Someone checks the calendar.
Someone packs lunches.

Sometimes people rush.
Sometimes someone forgets a backpack.

But voices stay steady.

If someone feels frustrated, they say it.
They do not yell.
They do not swear.

If they mess up, they stop.
They take a breath.
They say sorry.
They fix it.

I heard that.

My sister eats slowly.
She talks about her dreams.
She does not watch adult faces.

My brother keeps one headphone off.
He stays at the table longer.

I breathe easier.

At Dad and Stormy's house, mornings feel louder and faster.

Doors close hard.
Phones buzz.
People talk over each other.

Sometimes everyone is running late.
Sometimes someone is already frustrated.

Words come out quickly.
Sometimes adults talk about each other like no one else is listening.

But we are.

Max stays close to me.
He watches the room.
Blue hides under the bed.

My sister covers her ears.
She asks, "Is someone mad?"

My brother leaves the room.
He puts both headphones on.
He disappears.

I stay very still.

After school it feels different too.

At Mom and Ozzie's house, someone asks how my day was.
They listen to the answer.

Homework happens at the table.
If someone gets stuck, they help.
If someone gets tired, they take a break.

At Dad and Stormy's house, afternoons feel rushed.

Phones ring.
Plans change.

Sometimes no one asks about school.
Sometimes someone is too upset to listen.

Dinner feels different.

At one house, dinner happens at the table.
People sit.
They talk about their day.

At the other house, dinner happens whenever.
Sometimes in the car.
Sometimes in front of a screen.

At Mom and Ozzie's house, rules stay the same.
Bedtime is bedtime.

At Dad and Stormy's house, sometimes it feels like they are trying very hard to make things fun — like they are afraid we might not want to be there.

I do not always know what to expect.

At night, I think about the next day.

I think about which house I will be in.
I think about how it will feel.

Some nights I fall asleep fast.
Some nights I don't.

## What I Saw

Kids notice patterns.
Tone matters more than explanations.
Consistency makes kids feel calm.
Animals react to stress before kids talk about it.

## What It Did to Me

My stomach hurts when voices change.
I watch the dog to know if I should be scared.
I help my sister calm down.
I wonder why my brother disappears.
I feel tired — even after sleeping.

## I Learned Something

Calm feels different than quiet.
Yelling stays in my body.
Adults choose their words.
Kids remember everything.
Safety shows up in routines.

## What This Story Shows

Kids do not need perfect parents.
They need steady ones.

When adults cannot make marriage work,
kids still need adults to make co-parenting work.

Kids should not have to choose sides.
They should not carry adult words.
They should not feel responsible for adult emotions.

Kids just want to be kids.

Chapter 2

# Questions Kids Should Not Have to Answer

Sometimes adults ask questions.

They do not sound like questions.
They sound like tests.

I am ten.

I know when a question is safe.
And I know when it is not.

Safe questions sound like this:

"How was school?"
"What made you laugh today?"
"Do you want a snack?"

Safe questions feel light.
They do not have the right answer.

Unsafe questions feel different.

They come quickly.
They come quietly.
They come when adults think kids are not paying attention.

At Mom and Ozzie's house, questions feel simple.

They ask about homework.
They ask about friends.
They ask if I slept well.

If I say I don’t know,
that is okay.

If I do not want to talk,
that is okay too.

At Dad and Stormy’s house, some questions feel heavier.

They come when we are driving.
They come when the radio is off.
They come when adults sound tense.

“Did your mom really say that?”
“Your dad doesn’t tell you the whole truth.”
“Which house do you like better?”

My stomach tightens.

I look out the window.
I pretend I did not hear.

Sometimes adults say,
“I’m just asking.”

But it does not feel that way.

My sister listens to the questions too.

She does not understand all the words.
But she understands the feeling.

She gets quiet.
Later she asks, “Is someone mad?”

My brother hears the questions.

He rolls his eyes.
He puts on his headphones.

But later, I heard him pacing in his room.

Questions follow me.

They follow me to practice.

They follow me to school.
They follow me to bed.

I think about what the right answer is.

I think about who might get upset.

Sometimes I tell the truth.

Sometimes I change it a little.

Sometimes I say nothing at all.

I wish adults knew this:

When they ask me to explain something to the other parent,
or to repeat what was said,
or to compare houses —

It feels like they are asking me to choose.

I do not want to choose.

I want to be a kid.

## What I Saw

Adults sometimes use questions to manage their own feelings.
Kids feel the pressure even when voices stay calm.
Questions can quietly turn kids into messengers.

## What It Did to Me

My stomach hurt when questions came.
I felt responsible for adult emotions.
I worried about saying the wrong thing.
I started thinking before speaking — all the time.

## I Learned Something

Some questions are not meant for kids.
Silence can feel safer than honesty.
Choosing sides hurts — even when no one says that is what they are asking.

## What This Story Shows

Kids should not be asked to explain adult conflicts.
Kids should not be put in the middle.
Adults need to talk to adults.

When adults protect children from divided loyalty,
children feel safer in both homes.

# Chapter 3
# Loud Words and Quiet Kids

They are not always shouted.
But they feel loud.

I know when loud words are coming.

My body knows before my ears do.

My shoulders tighten.
My stomach feels strange.
The room feels smaller.

At Mom and Ozzie's house, voices change.

They get firm.
They get serious.
But they do not explode.

When someone gets upset, they say,
"I need a minute."
or
"This isn't the right time."

The dog, Max, stays where he is.
The cat, Blue, does not move.

The room stays steady.

At Dad and Stormy's house, loud words come faster.

They jump out.
They fill the room.
Sometimes sharp words come with them.

My sister covers her ears.

She starts to cry.

My brother disappears.
He shuts his door.

I stay very still.

No one asks us to leave.
No one says,
"This is adult talk."

We hear everything.

Sometimes the loud words are about money.
Sometimes they are about schedules.
Sometimes they are about the other parent.
Sometimes they are about things that don't even seem big.

But they feel big.

At Mom and Ozzie's house, if voices rise too high, they stop.

They notice us.
They say,
"Sorry you heard that."

They lower their voices.

The room settles again.

At Dad and Stormy's house, sometimes no one notices.

The loud words keep going.

Sometimes adults say,
"This is just how people talk."
or
"You'll be fine."

I learned something.

We are not fine.

## What I Saw

Loud words change how a room feels.
Tone matters more than explanations.
Kids listen to volume, not reasons.
Animals react when voices rise.

## What It Did to Me

My heart beats fast.
I listen for footsteps.
I learn where to sit.
I learn when to be quiet.
I help my sister calm down.
I wonder when it will stop.

## I Learned Something

Yelling does not teach strength.
It teaches alertness.

Calm voices teach safety.
Stopping teaches control.

When adults lose control with words,
kids learn how to disappear.

## What This Story Shows

Children do not need adults who never get upset.
They need adults who know how to pause.

When adults regulate themselves,
kids relax.

When adults stay steady —
even in frustration —
kids feel safe.

This is when I started listening
more than talking.

## Something I Noticed Later

I noticed my body reacted
before my thoughts did.

My heart beat faster.
My stomach hurt.

No one explained this to me.

It just happened.

# Chapter 4
# Secrets Kids Should Not Have to Keep

Some secrets are surprises.

Those are fun.

But some secrets feel heavy.

I know the difference.

At Mom and Ozzie's house, secrets are small.

"Don't tell your sister about her birthday cake."
"Close your eyes."

They always end up smiling.

At Dad & Stormy's house, secrets feel different.

They come with warnings.

"Don't tell your mom."
"Don't tell your dad."
"These stays between us."

When adults say that my chest feels tight.

My sister is five.
She nods even when she does not understand.

My brother is fifteen.
He gets quiet.
He looks tired.

I am ten.
I try to remember everything,
so I don't mess up.

Sometimes the secret is about money.
Sometimes it is about court.
Sometimes it is about the other parent.

Sometimes it is about nothing that should be secret at all.

At Mom and Ozzie's house, no one asks us to hide things.

They talk to each other.
They handle adult problems.

They do not put them in our pockets.

At Dad & Stormy's house, secrets pile up.

I carry them to school.
I carry them to bed.

I worry I will say the wrong thing.

The dog, Max, stays close.
The cat, Blue, leaves the room.

## I learned something

Sometimes adults say,
"I'm just protecting you."

But it does not feel like protection.

It feels like pressure.

## What I Saw

Adults used secrets to control feelings.
Kids were asked to hold adult problems.
Secrets made kids anxious, not safe.
Animals reacted to the tension.

## What It Did to Me

My stomach hurt.
I worried about talking.
I felt nervous around both parents.
I tried to remember rules that kept changing.
I felt responsible for keeping peace.

## What This Story Shows

Kids should not be asked to keep adult secrets.
Kids should not be asked to hide information.
Kids should not be asked to protect adults.

Adults need to talk to adults.

When adults use kids to hold secrets,
kids lose a sense of safety.

Kids need honesty that feels safe,
not secrets that feel heavy.

# Chapter 5
# When Rules Change to Win

I think sometimes adults change rules because they feel bad about what kids lost.
They want to give something back.

But it still makes my stomach hurt.

Rules are supposed to help.

They tell you what to do.
They help you feel safe.

I learned that rules feel different in different houses.

At Mom and Ozzie's house, rules stay the same.

Bedtime is bedtime.
Homework comes before screens.
Dinner happens at the table.

If a rule changes, they explain why.

At Dad & Stormy's house, rules change fast.

They change depending on who is mad.
They change to make someone happy.
They change to prove a point.

Sometimes I hear,
"You don't have to follow that rule here."
"Your mom is too strict."
"Your dad doesn't know what he's doing."

My sister smiles when rules disappear.

But later she cries.

My brother shrugs.
He stops caring.

I feel confused.

At Mom and Ozzie's house, rules are boring.

But boring feels calm.

At Dad & Stormy's house, rules feel like prizes.

They come and go.

I learned something
Sometimes rules change before birthdays.
Sometimes they change before visits.
Sometimes they change just to win.

The dog, Max, does better with routines.
The cat, Blue, likes knowing where to sit.

So do we.

## What I Saw

Rules were used to compete.
Kids were caught in the middle.
Consistency made kids feel calm.
Changing rules created confusion.

## What It Did to Me

I did not know what was expected.
I worried about doing the wrong thing.
I learned different rules for different people.
I felt anxious instead of safe.

## What This Story Shows

Kids need rules they can trust.
Rules should not be used to compete.
Rules should not be changed to win.

When adults undermine each other,
kids lose stability.

Kids do better when adults agree,
even if they live in two houses.

## Chapter 6
# When Kids Become the Messenger

Sometimes adults do not talk to each other.

They talk through kids.

I am ten.
I know when a message is not mine.

At Mom and Ozzie's house, messages go to adults.

They text.
They email.
They talk.

They do not use us.

At Dad & Stormy's house, messages land on us.

"Tell your mom the schedule changed."
"Tell your dad I'm not paying for that."
"Make sure they know I said no."

My sister is five.
She repeats things wrong.
She gets in trouble.

My brother is fifteen.
He says nothing.
He lets adults argue later.

I try to say it right.

I practice the words in my head.

Sometimes the message is angry.
Sometimes it is cold.
Sometimes it is meant to hurt.

I do not want to carry it.

At Mom and Ozzie's house, adults say,
"That's not your job."

They protect us from the middle.

At Dad & Stormy's house, adults say,
"It's not a big deal."

But it feels big.

The dog, Max, walks back and forth.
The cat, Blue, leaves the room.

## I learned something

Sometimes the message changes how visits feel.

Sometimes it changes how dinner feels.

Sometimes it changes how I feel about both houses.

## What I Saw

Adults avoided talking to each other.
Kids were used as delivery.
Messages carried anger.
Kids were blamed when messages went wrong.

## What It Did to Me

I felt nervous before visits.
I worried about saying it wrong.
I felt responsible for adult reactions.
I wished adults would talk to adults.

## What This Story Shows

Kids should not be messengers.
Kids should not carry adult conflict.
Kids should not be in the middle.

When adults talk through kids,
kids feel pressure instead of peace.

Co-parenting works better
when adults communicate directly.

Sometimes I wanted to say,
"Please talk to each other,"
but I didn't know how.

## Something I Noticed Later

I noticed that carrying messages
made visits feel heavier.

Even when the words were quiet,
they stayed loud in my head.

# Chapter 7
# When Apologies Do Not Come

Sometimes adults mess up.

Everyone does.

But what happens next matters.

I am ten.
I notice when apologies come.
And when they do not.

At Mom and Ozzie's house, mistakes slow things down.

Someone raises a voice.
Someone says something sharp.

Then things get quiet.

Later, I hear,
"I shouldn't have said that."
"I'm sorry you heard that."
"I was wrong."

They do not make excuses.
They do not blame.

They just say it.

My sister relaxes.
My brother comes back.
The dog, Max, stretches out.
The cat, Blue, stays.

At Dad & Stormy's house, mistakes move fast.

Yelling happens.
Doors close.

Then everything goes back to normal.

No one talks about it.
No one says sorry.

Sometimes adults say,
"That's just how I am."
or
"You're too sensitive."

My sister stays quiet.
My brother stays gone.

I will stay careful.

I do not know if it is over.
I do not know if it will happen again.

## I learned something.

At Mom and Ozzie's house, apologies feel like safety.

They tell us,
"This is not your fault."

At Dad & Stormy's house, silence feels heavy.

It tells us,
"Get used to it."

## What I Saw

Mistakes were handled differently.
Apologies brought calm.
Silence brought fear.
Kids watched what adults did next.

## What It Did to Me

I waited for things to explode again.
I learned not to expect repair.
I felt unsure even when things were quiet.
I wished someone would say sorry.

## What This Story Shows

Kids need repair after making mistakes.
Apologies help kids feel safe.
Silence does not heal.

When adults refuse to repair,
kids stay alert.

Kids trust adults who can say,
"I was wrong."

# Chapter 8
# When Calm Feels Boring --and Safe

Some days I feel quiet.

Not exciting.
Not loud.

Just quiet.

I am ten.
I used to think calm was boring.

At Mom and Ozzie's house, not much happens.

We eat.
We do homework.
We sit.

Max sleeps.
Blue stays on the chair.

No one slams doors.
No one yells.

At first, it felt strange.

I waited for something to happen.

At Dad & Stormy's house, something is always happening.

Voices rise.
Phones buzz.
Plans change.

Sometimes it feels exciting.

Sometimes it feels scary.

My sister asks,
"Are they mad?"

My brother keeps his headphones on.

I watch the room.

At Mom and Ozzie's house, calm stays.

If someone gets upset, they breathe.
They talk later.

Nothing explodes.

Max stretches.
Blue stays.

I learned something
I started to like calm.

I started to feel sleepy in a good way.

At Dad & Stormy's house, calm never lasts.

When it is quiet, it feels fake.

I wait for the next loud moment.

## What I Saw

Calm did not mean nothing was happening.
Calm meant adults were in control.
Noise felt exciting but unsafe.
Quiet felt steady.

## What It Did to Me

I could focus.
I could rest.
I did not watch the door.
I did not worry as much.

## What This Story Shows

Kids do not need excitement.
They need safety.

Calm homes help kids relax.
Calm adults help kids feel safe.

When calm feels boring,
it is usually because peace is new.

Peace is not boring.

Peace is safe.

# Chapter 9
# When Kids Pretend, They Are Fine

Most of the time, adults ask,
"Are you okay?"

I know how to answer that.

I am ten.
I say,
"I'm fine."

My sister is five.
She nods.

My brother is fifteen.
He shrugs.

At Mom and Ozzie's house, someone notices.

They look at our faces.
They ask again later.

They say,
"You don't seem fine."

Sometimes I cry.
Sometimes my sister talks.
Sometimes my brother sits down.

At Dad & Stormy's house, "fine" ends the talk.

No one looks closer.

Sometimes adults say,
"You're strong."
or
"You'll get over it."

So, we stop trying.

## I learned something

I learned how to smile.
I learned how to say okay.
I learned how to keep things inside.

The dog, Max, stays near.
The cat, Blue, watches from far away.

At Mom and Ozzie's house, being honest feels safe.

At Dad & Stormy's house, being honest feels risky.

## What I Saw

Kids learned to hide feelings.
Adults missed quiet signals.
Being fine meant being unseen.

## What It Did to Me

My chest felt heavy.
I kept things inside.
I felt lonely even with people around.
I wondered if my feelings mattered.

## What This Story Shows

Kids pretend they are fine to survive.
Kids open-up when it feels safe.

Adults need to look past the word “fine.”
They need to slow down.

When adults notice feelings,
kids feel seen.

Feeling seen helps kids heal.

## Something I Noticed Later

I noticed calm didn't feel boring anymore.

It felt like rest.

I didn't watch the room as much.
I didn't listen for doors.

This is where I learned
how to look okay
even when I wasn't.

# Chapter 10
# When Kids Feel Responsible

Sometimes I feel like it is my job to fix things.

No one tells me that.
But I feel it anyway.

I am ten.
I notice when adults are upset.

At Mom and Ozzie's house, adults handle feelings.

If someone is stressed, they say it.
If someone is mad, they take a break.

They do not look at us to make it better.

At Dad & Stormy's house, feelings spill.

When someone is upset, the room feels tight.
Eyes turn toward us.

My sister tries to be extra good.
She cleans up fast.
She hugs people.

My brother tries to stay out of the way.
He stays in his room.
He leaves early.

I try to help.

I listen.
I stay quiet.
I do what I am told.

Sometimes adults say,
"Don't upset your mom."
or
"Be nice so your dad doesn't get mad."

I feel like it is on me.

At Mom and Ozzie's house, they say,
"This is not your job."

They mean it.

At Dad & Stormy's house, no one says that.

So. I keep trying.

### I learned something

The dog, Max, follows moods.
The cat, Blue, disappears.

### What I Saw

Kids watched adult emotions.
Kids tried to manage adult moods.
Adults did not notice the weight.

## What It Did to Me

I worried a lot.
I felt tense.
I felt older than ten.
I forgot how to relax.

## What This Story Shows

Kids should not feel responsible for adult emotions.
Kids should not try to keep peace.

Adults are responsible for their feelings.
Adults are responsible for the home.

When adults take responsibility,
kids can be kids.

# Chapter 11
# When Repair Changes Things

Not everything remains broken.

I did not know that at first.

I am ten.
I thought once something went wrong,
it stayed that way.

At Mom and Ozzie's house, repairs happen.

Someone says something they should not.
Someone gets loud.

Then later, something else happens.

They came back.

They say,
"I was wrong."
"I'm sorry."
"That was not okay."

They do not blame.
They do not rush.

My sister relaxes.
My brother comes back.
The room feels lighter.

The dog, Max, stretches out.
The cat, Blue, stays close.

At Dad & Stormy's house, things move on.

No one comes back.
No one talks about it.

The yelling is over,
but the feeling stays.

I do not know if it will happen again.
I do not know if it is safe yet.

At Mom and Ozzie's house, repair tells us,
"This will not be ignored."

It tells us,
"You matter."

At Dad & Stormy's house, silence tells us,
"Get used to it."

## I learned something

It is not the yelling that scares me most.

It is not knowing what comes next.

## What I Saw

Repair changed how the house felt.
Words mattered after mistakes.
Coming back made a difference.

## What It Did to Me

I trusted more.
I relaxed faster.
I did not stay on alert as long.
I felt safer in my body.

## What This Story Shows

Repair helps kids feel safe again.
Repair teaches kids mistakes can be fixed.

Saying sorry is not weakness.
It is protection.

When adults repair,
kids learn trust.

When adults return after conflict,
kids learn they matter.

## Chapter 12

# When Kids Start to Feel Safe Again

Safety does not come all at once.

It comes slowly.

I am ten.
I did not trust calm right away.

At first, when things were quiet,
I waited.

I watched faces.
I listened to voices.

At Mom and Ozzie's house, they stayed calm.

Days passed.
Nothing exploded.

They kept routines.
They kept rules.
They kept coming back.

My sister slept better.
She stopped crying at night.

My brother stayed longer.
He took off his headphones sometimes.

The dog, Max, stopped pacing.
The cat, Blue, stayed in the room.

At Dad & Stormy's house, calm came and went.

Sometimes things were good.
Sometimes they were not.

I stayed ready.

At Mom and Ozzie's house, safety grew.

It grew in small ways.

In dinners.
In mornings.
In boring days.

### I learned something

Safety is not loud.

Safety is steady.

### What I Saw

Safety showed up through consistency.
Time mattered.
Kids noticed patterns.

## What It Did to Me

I breathed easier.
I slept deeper.
I laughed more.
I felt like a kid again.

## What This Story Shows

Kids feel safe when adults are predictable.
Safety grows through steady actions.

Kids do not need big promises.
They need adults who keep showing up.

Feeling safe again takes time.
But it is possible.

Something felt different here.
Not loud.
Not exciting.
Just safer.

## Something I Noticed Later

I noticed I trusted adults more
after they came back.

Not because they were perfect.

Because they didn't disappear.

# Chapter 13
# When Trust Grows Slowly

Trust does not come back fast.

It comes in pieces.

I am ten.
I did not trust again right away.

At first, when things felt calm,
I waited.

I watched faces.
I listened to voices.
I looked for signs.

At Mom and Ozzie's house, they stayed steady.

They did not rush us.
They did not say,
"See, everything is fine now."

They just kept going.

Days turned into weeks.

No yelling.
No bad words.
No secrets.

My sister laughed more.
She stopped asking if people were mad.

My brother stayed longer.
He talked more.
He stopped leaving so fast.

The dog, Max, slept deeply.
The cat, Blue, stayed close.

At Dad & Stormy's house, trust was harder.

Sometimes things were good.
Sometimes they were not.

I learned not to expect too much.

At Mom and Ozzie's house, trust grew quietly.

It grew when adults did what they said.
It grew when rules stayed the same.
It grew when apologies kept coming.

## I learned something

Trust grows when adults are predictable.

## What I Saw

Trust returned through repeated actions.
Time mattered more than words.
Kids watched what happened next.

## What It Did to Me

I stopped waiting for things to fall apart.
I relaxed my shoulders.
I believed calm could last.

## What This Story Shows

Trust takes time.
Kids rebuild trust through consistency.

Adults cannot rush healing.
They must earn it.

When adults stay steady,
trust grows.

# Chapter 14
# When Kids Believe Change is Real

At first, I thought change was a trick.

I had seen promises before.

I am ten.
I learned to wait before believing.

At Mom and Ozzie's house, change stayed.

Not for a day.
Not for a week.

It stayed through bad moods.
It stayed through hard days.

When someone got upset, they handled it.
When someone messed up, they fixed it.

They kept coming back.

My sister stopped asking,
"Is someone mad?"

My brother stopped leaving so fast.

The dog, Max, slept without moving.
The cat, Blue, stayed on the couch.

At Dad & Stormy's house, change came and went.

Some days were better.
Some days were not.

I learned not to count on it.

## I learned something

At Mom and Ozzie's house, something new happened.

I stopped waiting for the next problem.
I stopped watching faces all the time.

I believed calm could last.

## What I Saw

Change was shown through actions.
Consistency mattered more than words.
Kids noticed patterns over time.

## What It Did to Me

I trusted again.
I relaxed.
I felt lighter.
I felt hopeful.

## What This Story Shows

Kids believe change when it lasts.
Kids need adults to show growth, not talk about it.

Change becomes real when adults keep choosing it,
even when it is hard.

# Chapter 15
# When School Becomes the Place it Comes Out

I am ten.

School is where I am supposed to behave.
That is what adults say.

But sometimes school is where everything spills out.

At school, no one knows which house I came from that morning.
No one knows if I slept.
No one knows if voices were loud.
No one knows if rules changed again.

They just see me.

Sometimes I am quiet.
Too quiet.

I stare at my paper.
I forget directions.
I forget what the teacher just said.

Sometimes I get in trouble.
I talk back.
I snap at kids.
I get frustrated fast.

Sometimes I cry over small things.
Sometimes I don't care at all.

Adults at school say,
"That behavior came out of nowhere."

But it didn't.

It came from remembering two schedules.
Two sets of rules.
Two ways of being careful.

At one house, mornings are calm.
At the other house, mornings feel rushed.

When I get to school, my body is still catching up.

Sometimes I forget my homework.
Not because I didn't do it.
But because it stayed in the other house.

I am not trying to be bad.
I am trying to hold it together.

## What I Saw

Kids carried home stress into school.
Teachers saw behavior, not the cause.
Transitions between houses affected focus and mood.

## What It Did to Me

I felt embarrassed when I got in trouble.
I felt confused when adults didn't understand.
I worried school would think I was a bad kid.

## What This Story Shows

Behavior is communication.
Kids from two households may act out at school not because they are defiant,
but because they are overwhelmed.

Kids do better when adults ask,
"What happened before this?"
instead of,
"What's wrong with you?"

# Chapter 16
# When Home Feels Like Home Again

Home did not feel safe right away.

It came back slowly.

I am ten.
I forgot what home was supposed to feel like.

At first, houses were just places.

Places to sleep.
Places to wait.
Places to leave.

At Mom and Ozzie's house, something changed.

Not in one big moment.
In small ones.

Dinner felt easier.
Mornings felt normal.
Silence did not scare me.

My sister laughed without checking faces.
She played on the floor.

My brother stayed longer.
He joked sometimes.
He stopped standing near the door.

The dog, Max, slept wherever he wanted.
The cat, Blue, stayed nearby.

I noticed I stopped counting time.

I stopped waiting to leave.

At Dad & Stormy's house, home still felt shaky.

Some days were good.
Some days were not.

But now I know the difference.

I learned something
Home was not noisy.
Home was not gifts.
Home was not pretending.

Home was calm.

## What I Saw

Home returned through consistency.
Safety made space for joy.
Kids noticed when peace lasted.

## What It Did to Me

I felt settled.
I felt lighter.
I felt like I belonged.

## What This Story Shows

Home feels like home when kids feel safe.
Safety grows through steady care.

Kids do not need perfect homes.
They need calm ones.

## Something I Noticed Later

I noticed school felt easier
when mornings were calm.

My body arrived before my worries did.

# Chapter 17
# When Kids Feel Free to be Kids

Being a kid used to feel heavy.

I did not know that at first.

I am ten.
I thought this was just how life was.

At first, I worried about things kids should not worry about.

Who was mad.
What would happen next.
What I should say.

At Mom and Ozzie's house, something changed.

I started playing.

I laughed without checking the room.
I forgot to listen to voices.

My sister played on the floor.
She made messes.
She did not apologize for them.

My brother relaxed.
He stayed longer.
He smiled more.

The dog, Max, chased his tail.
The cat, Blue, stretched in the sun.

No one told us to stop worrying.

We just stopped.

At Dad & Stormy's house, being a kid still felt careful.

I stayed alert.
I stayed quiet.

But now I knew it did not have to be that way.

## I learned something

Being a kid meant laughing.
Being a kid meant playing.
Being a kid meant not fixing things.

## What I Saw

Kids returned to play when they felt safe.
Joy showed up naturally.
Adults did not force it.

## What It Did to Me

I felt lighter.
I laughed more.
I stopped carrying adult problems.
I felt my age again.

## What This Story Shows

Kids thrive when they feel safe.
Safety gives kids permission to be kids.

Adults create the space.
Kids fill it with life.

# Chapter 18
# When Adults Choose the Child First

Sometimes adults have choices.

They do not always say them out loud.
But kids can feel them.

I am ten.
I notice when adults choose me.

At Mom and Ozzie's house, choices feel quiet.

Someone pauses.
Someone takes a breath.
Someone stops a sentence before it gets sharp.

They do not try to win.
They do not try to be right.

They choose calm.

Sometimes it means an adult walks away.
Sometimes it means they say,
"This can wait."

When that happens, my body relaxes.

At Dad & Stormy's house, choices feel rushed.

Words come out fast.
Feelings spill.

Winning feels important.
Being heard feels urgent.

Sometimes adults say,
"I deserve to say how I feel."

But kids feel the cost.

My sister freezes.
My brother leaves.
I stay quiet.

At Mom and Ozzie's house, adults say,
"This is about the kids."

And they mean it.

They choose peace over pride.
They choose repair over silence.
They choose us over the argument.

The dog, Max, lies down.
The cat, Blue, stays close.

## I learned something

Adults always choose something.

Kids live with that choice.

## What I Saw

Adults paused before reacting.
Choices protected kids.
Calm was chosen on purpose.

## What It Did to Me

I felt valued.
I felt protected.
I trusted adults more.

## What This Story Shows

Kids feel safe when adults choose them.
Putting kids first changes everything.

Adults do not have to agree.
They have to protect.

Choosing the child first
creates peace that lasts.

I didn't need things to be perfect.
I just needed adults
to stay.

## Monday

Mondays feel rushed.
I check my backpack twice.
I forget things even when I try not to.

I wonder what kind of day it will be.
I wonder who will be upset.
I try to be ready for everything.

## Tuesday

Tuesdays feel unsure.
I listen carefully to every voice.
I watch for small changes.

If someone sighs, I notice.
If someone walks fast, I notice.
I try to stay small so nothing gets bigger.

## Wednesday

Wednesdays feel quieter.
I stop watching faces.
I breathe without thinking about it.

My shoulders drop a little.
I don't feel like I have to solve anything.
I just do my work.

## THURSDAY

Thursdays feel heavy.
I think about tomorrow.
I think about what might shift.

I pack more than I need.
I say less than I want.
I prepare inside, just in case.

## FRIDAY

Fridays feel lighter.
I laugh easier.
I forget what I was worried about.

My body feels softer.
I don't plan escape routes.
I just play.

## SATURDAY

Saturdays feel steady.
No one is rushing.
No one is checking the clock.

I stay where I am.
I don't brace for noise.
I feel normal.

## SUNDAY

Sundays feel calm.
I don't count time.
I don't wait for things to change.

I rest.
I don't prepare for impact.
I just live inside the day.

# Chapter 19
# When Co-Parenting Starts to Work

I did not know co-parenting could feel different.

I thought it was always hard.

I am ten.
I notice when adults work together.

At Mom and Ozzie's house, things feel smoother.

Schedules stay the same.
Rules match.
Messages go to adults.

I do not hear bad things about the other house.
I do not get asked questions I cannot answer.

Adults talk without us.

At Dad & Stormy's house, co-parenting feels rough.

Plans change.
Rules clash.
Messages come through kids.

I feel pulled.

At Mom and Ozzie's house, co-parenting feels boring.

But boring feels good.

I know what to expect.
I know where I am going.
I know what the rules are.

My sister stops asking,
"What day is it?"

My brother stops, checking his phone.

The dog, Max, follows routines.
The cat, Blue, stays nearby.

### I learned something

Co-parenting works when adults talk.
It works when kids are not in the middle.

### What I saw

Consistency, helped kids relax.
Adult communication mattered.
Kids noticed when things matched.

## What It Did to Me

I felt settled.
I worried less.
I trusted the schedule.
I felt calm.

## What This Story Shows

Co-parenting works when adults cooperate.
Kids should not manage schedules or feelings.

When adults align,
kids feel secure.

Working together gives kids peace.

# Chapter 20
# When Both Houses Feel Predictable

I used to feel different in each house.

I did not know what version of life I was walking into.

I am ten.
I notice when things match.

At first, days felt uneven.

One house felt calm.
The other felt unsure.

Then something changed.

At Mom and Ozzie's house, routines stayed.
At the other house, routines started to stay too.

Rules did not shift.
Bedtime stayed bedtime.
School nights stayed quiet.

I stopped asking,
"What are we doing tonight?"

I stopped wondering,
"Is this okay here?"

My sister stopped checking faces.
She followed the routine.

My brother stopped watching the clock.
He settled in.

The dog, Max, knew where to sleep.
The cat, Blue, stayed close.

## I learned something

Predictable does not mean boring.

Predictable means safe.

## What I Saw

Consistency helped both houses feel steady.
Matching routines reduced stress.
Kids noticed when expectations stayed the same.

## What It Did to Me

I relaxed.
I trusted both homes.
I stopped bracing for change.
I felt secure.

## What This Story Shows

Kids thrive on predictability.
Two steady houses are better than one.

When adults align,
kids feel safe everywhere.

# Chapter 21
# When Adults Keep Their Word

Words are easy to say.

Keeping them is harder.

I am ten.
I notice when words match actions.

At first, I heard a lot of promises.

"It will be better."
"I won't do that again."
"Things are changing."

Sometimes they were true.
Sometimes they were not.

At Mom and Ozzie's house, promises stayed small.

They did not promise big things.
They promised simple things.

"We'll pick you up at six."
"We'll talk later."
"I'll be there."

And then they were.

Time passed.
They kept doing what they said.

My sister stopped asking,
"Are they really coming?"

My brother stopped checking his phone.

The dog, Max, waited calmly.
The cat, Blue, did not move.

At the other house, words sometimes changed.

Plans shifted.
Times moved.
Explanations came later.

## I learned something

Big promises did not make me feel safe.
Kept promises did.

## What I Saw

Kids watched for follow-through.
Actions mattered more than words.
Small promises-built trust.

## What It Did to Me

I trusted adults more.
I stopped worrying about being forgotten.
I felt secure.

## What This Story Shows

Kids feel safe when adults keep their word.
Trust grows through follow-through.

Adults do not need perfect plans.
They need reliable ones.

Keeping promises
protects kids.

# Chapter 22
# When Stability Feels Real --and Normal

At first, I kept asking myself a question.

I did not say it out loud.

I am ten.

I wondered,
"Is this real?"

When things stayed calm,
I waited for them to change.

When adults kept their word,
I waited for them to forget.

I had learned to expect the shift.

At Mom and Ozzie's house, the shift did not come.

Days went by.
Weeks went by.

Rules stayed the same.
Voices stayed steady.
Promises were kept.

No one made a big announcement about it.

It just stayed.

I stopped asking the question.

My sister stopped checking faces.
She stopped asking if someone was mad.

My brother stopped bracing for problems.
He stayed at the table.
He laughed more.

The dog, Max, slept deeply.
The cat, Blue, stretched out in the open.

The house felt settled.

And so, did I.

Stability started to feel normal.

I did not celebrate it.
I did not talk about it.

I just lived in it.

At the other house, things were still uneven.

Some days were good.
Some days felt rushed.
Some days voices rose.

But now I knew what steady felt like.

And that mattered.

Stability was not exciting.
It was not loud.
It did not need to prove anything.

Stability was calm.

Stability meant I did not have to think so much.
I did not have to watch.
I did not have to wait.

My body stopped staying ready.

I learned something.

When stability is real,
kids stop asking if it will last.

They begin to trust tomorrow.

## What I Saw

Stability showed up through time.
Normal routines created safety.
Consistency mattered more than promises.
Kids noticed when calm stayed.

## What It Did to Me

I felt grounded.
I trusted the days.
I stopped waiting for things to fall apart.
I slept deeper.

## What This Story Shows

Kids heal when stability becomes normal.

Safety does not need to be announced.
It needs to be repeated.

When adults stay steady,
kids believe it.

And when kids believe it,
they finally rest.

And when they finally rest,
they begin to grow.

This is what I wish
someone would have noticed sooner.

# PART II

## Reflection for Adults

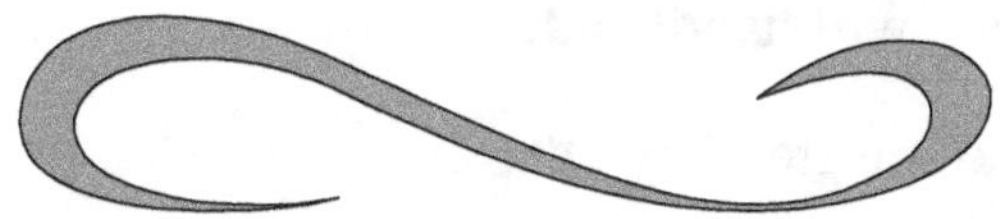

# Closing Chapter
# A Note to the Adults Who Care for Me

You may have read this book looking for answers.
Or reassurance.
Or proof that you are doing the best you can.

You may have read it feeling defensive, sad, tired, convicted, or hopeful.

This book was not written to judge you.

It was written to show you what children experience.

Children do not see court orders.
They do not hear intentions.
They do not understand legal language.

They feel tone.
They notice patterns.
They remember what happens after mistakes.

Most children want the same things:

- To feel safe in both homes
- To love both parents without pressure
- To stay out of adult conflict
- To trust that adults will handle adult problems

When children feel unsafe, they adapt.

They get quiet.
They get loud.
They disappear.
They try to fix things.
They pretend they are fine.

These are not character flaws.

They are survival skills.

What children need most is not perfection.

They need predictability.
They need repair.
They need adults who can pause instead of react.

Children do not need parents to agree on everything.

They need parents to protect them from conflict.

Co-parenting does not require friendship.

It requires responsibility.

Every calm response teaches safety.
Every apology teaches trust.
Every boundary that keeps children out of the middle teaches protection.

Change does not happen in one conversation.

Children believe change when it lasts.

If you take nothing else from this book, remember this:

Children feel safest when adults choose them first —
before pride,
before proving a point,
before reacting.

When adults change how they speak, respond, and cooperate,
children feel the difference immediately.

And when children feel safe,
they finally get to be children again.

And it is not too late to begin.

# TOOLS FOR ADULTS

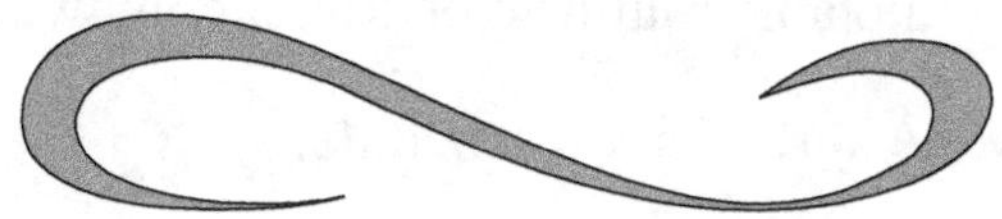

## HEALTHY CO-PARENTING CHECKLIST

*Protecting the Child's Experience*

### COMMUNICATION

- ☐ I do NOT use my child as a messenger.
- ☐ I communicate directly with the other parent.
- ☐ I keep my tone calm and neutral.
- ☐ I avoid asking my child questions meant for adults.
- ☐ I do not criticize the other parent in front of my child.

### EMOTIONAL SAFETY

- ☐ I manage my own emotions without expecting my child to comfort me.
- ☐ I do not react negatively when my child talks about the other home.
- ☐ I apologize when I raise my voice or make a mistake.
- ☐ I validate my child's feelings ("It's okay to feel that way").
- ☐ I stay steady, so my child doesn't have to guess my mood.

### ROUTINES & CONSISTENCY

- ☐ I keep predictable routines: bedtime, homework, meals.
- ☐ I follow the agreed-upon schedule.
- ☐ I maintain appropriate age boundaries.
- ☐ I do not change rules just to compete with the other home.
- ☐ I explain changes calmly when they are necessary.

### TRANSITIONS BETWEEN HOMES

- ☐ I keep drop-offs and pick-ups calm and brief.

- ☐ I send items needed to reduce stress.
- ☐ I avoid emotional conversations during transitions.
- ☐ I speak positively: “Have fun! See you soon!”
- ☐ I never make my child feel guilty for enjoying the other home.

**RESPECTING BOTH HOMES**

- ☐ I do not compare or rank the homes.
- ☐ I support reasonable rules in both households.
- ☐ I avoid asking “Which house do you like better?”
- ☐ I encourage healthy relationships with both parents.
- ☐ I focus on what I can control in my own home.

**REPAIR & RESPONSIBILITY**

- ☐ I admit when I am wrong.
- ☐ I repair quickly after conflict.
- ☐ I do not ignore or minimize my outbursts.
- ☐ I model calm problem-solving.
- ☐ I keep promises, especially small ones.

**STABILITY & TRUST**

- ☐ I maintain consistent expectations.
- ☐ I keep my word about pickups, times, and commitments.
- ☐ I ensure my child knows what to expect each day.
- ☐ I protect my child from adult conflict.
- ☐ I allow my child to be a kid—not a referee, negotiator, or secret keeper.

**THE DAILY PARENT PROMISE FOR THE CHILD**

*"Today, I choose my child first—before my frustration, before being right, and before the conflict."*

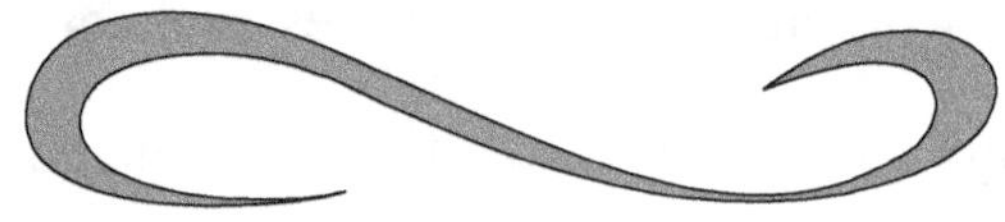

# Facilitator Appendix

***Guidance for Courts, Counselors, and Co-Parenting Programs***

*This material reflects common co-parenting patterns observed in clinical and court-adjacent settings and is not intended to assign fault to either parent.*

**Purpose of This Appendix**

This appendix is provided to support professionals using *Two Houses, One Childhood* in court-ordered or voluntary co-parenting education, mediation, or counseling settings.

The material is designed to:

- Promote insight without blame
- Increase child-focused awareness
- Reduce defensiveness
- Encourage behavioral change

**Suggested Session Pacing (Flexible)**

**Option A: 6–8 Session Model**

- 2–4 chapters per session
- Reflection + guided discussion
- No forced sharing

**Option B: 10–12 Session Model**

- 1–2 chapters per session
- Ideal for high-conflict cases
- Allows deeper reflection

**Option C: Individual or Self-Study**

- Assign chapters weekly
- Written reflection submitted
- Facilitator follow-up discussion

**Recommended Chapter Groupings**

**Session Group 1: The Child's World**

- Chapters 1–3
  *Two Houses, Questions, Loud Words*

**Focus:**
How children experience tone, conflict, and inconsistency

**Session Group 2: Being Put in the Middle**

- Chapters 4–6
  *Secrets, Rules, Messengers*

**Focus:**
How adult conflict transfers to children

**Session Group 3: Repair vs. Silence**

- Chapters 7–9
  *Apologies, Calm, Pretending*

**Focus:**
How repair builds safety and silence increases fear

**Session Group 4: Emotional Responsibility**

- Chapters 10–12
  *Responsibility, Repair, Safety*

**Focus:**
Who is responsible for emotions and healing

**Session Group 5: Trust & Stability**

- Chapters 13–15
  *Trust, Change, Consistency*

**Focus:**
How children rebuild trust over time

**Session Group 6: School, Home, and Growth**

- Chapters 16–18
  *School Behavior, Home, Being a Kid*

**Focus:**
How stress shows outside the home

**Session Group 7: Choosing the Child First**

- Chapters 19–23
  *Adult Choice, Cooperation, Stability*

**Focus:**
What effective co-parenting looks like in action

**Facilitator Reminders**

- Redirect from blame to impact
- Avoid adjudicating "who is right"
- Keep discussions child-focused
- Emphasize consistency over intention

Rapha
Christian Counseling Center

**CERTIFICATE OF COMPLETION**

# Two Houses, One Lonely Broken Heart

Divorce through the eyes of a ten year old

This certifies that:
**Parent/Participant Name:**______________________________

Has successfully completed the educational components associated with the resource:

## Two Houses, One Lonely Broken Heart

**Completion Includes:**

☐ Reading of all assigned chapters
☐ Engagement in structured reflection questions
☐ Review of the Healthy Co-Parenting Checklist
☐ Demonstrated awareness of child-focused co-parenting principles

**Completion Details**

Date Completed: ________
Case Number (if applicable): ________________________________

Parent/Participant Signature: ________________________________

**Facilitator Verification**
Facilitator Name: _________________________________
Agency / Program: _________________________________
Facilitator Signature: _______________________________
Date: ________

**Program Statement**
This certificate verifies educational participation and completion of program components. It does not constitute a custody evaluation, legal recommendation, or determination of parental fitness.

## Completion Summary

**For Court or Program Records**

This document verifies that the participant completed the educational components associated with *Two Houses, One Childhood: It's Not Too Late to Get This Right.*

Completion reflects engagement in the following areas:

**1. Assigned Reading**

The participant completed the required chapters addressing:

- The child's perspective in co-parenting dynamics
- The impact of tone, routine, and communication patterns
- The effects of unresolved conflict on child behavior
- The importance of emotional safety, repair, and consistency

**2. Reflection Components**

The participant engaged with structured reflection prompts, including:

- What I Saw
- What It Did to Me
- I Learned Something
- What This Story Shows

These prompts are designed to increase awareness of how adult behaviors influence child emotional experience.

**3. Healthy Co-Parenting Principles Reviewed**

The participants reviewed and discussed the Healthy Co-Parenting Checklist, including:

- Direct communication between parents
- Avoiding the use of children as messengers
- Maintaining predictable routines and consistency
- Demonstrating emotional regulation in the presence of children

**4. Trauma-Informed Awareness**

The participant demonstrated understanding of:

- Common signs of child stress and emotional overload
- Behavioral responses to divided loyalty or household inconsistency
- The importance of psychological and emotional safety

**5. Participation Component**

Participation included one or more of the following:

- Facilitated group sessions
- Individual review
- Guided discussion
- Written reflection or verbal processing

**Program Statement**

This summary verifies educational participation and completion of program components.

It does not constitute a custody evaluation, psychological assessment, legal recommendation, or determination of parental fitness.

## About the Author

**Dr. Janet Olivares** has devoted her life to Christian ministry and counseling, serving faithfully for many years with a heart for guiding people toward healing and wholeness in Christ. She is the founder of **Rapha Christian Counseling Center**, a ministry built on the belief that true transformation and restoration come only through the love and power of Jesus Christ.

Throughout her ministry journey, Dr. Olivares has walked alongside individuals, couples, and families facing some of life's most difficult challenges — from broken relationships and personal struggles to spiritual uncertainty and emotional pain. Her compassionate and Christ-centered approach has helped countless people find hope, healing, and the courage to rebuild their lives on God's Word.

As a counselor, teacher, and spiritual mentor, she is deeply committed to equipping others to discover their God-given identity and worth. She believes that every person is called to walk in freedom, joy, and intimacy with the Lord, and her passion is to see lives restored and transformed by the truth of Scripture and the power of prayer.

Through Rapha Christian Counseling Center, Dr. Olivares has created a safe space for people to encounter the grace of God, receive wise counsel, and find strength to face each season of life. Her ministry not only addresses the needs of the heart but also empowers believers to grow in faith, renew their minds, and embrace the abundant life promised in Christ.

## Be Sure to Check out my Other Titles:

Finding Self with God Day by Day
Forgive Let go for Real
Hooked and Confused
Suicide: Hope Beyond a Moment
Love Never Left: Marriage Restoration

How to contact the author:
*drjanet@raphaccc.org*

www.ingramcontent.com/pod-product-compliance
Lightning Source LLC
LaVergne TN
LVHW010627100826
845148LV00014B/3144

* 9 7 8 1 6 0 7 8 9 3 7 6 9 *